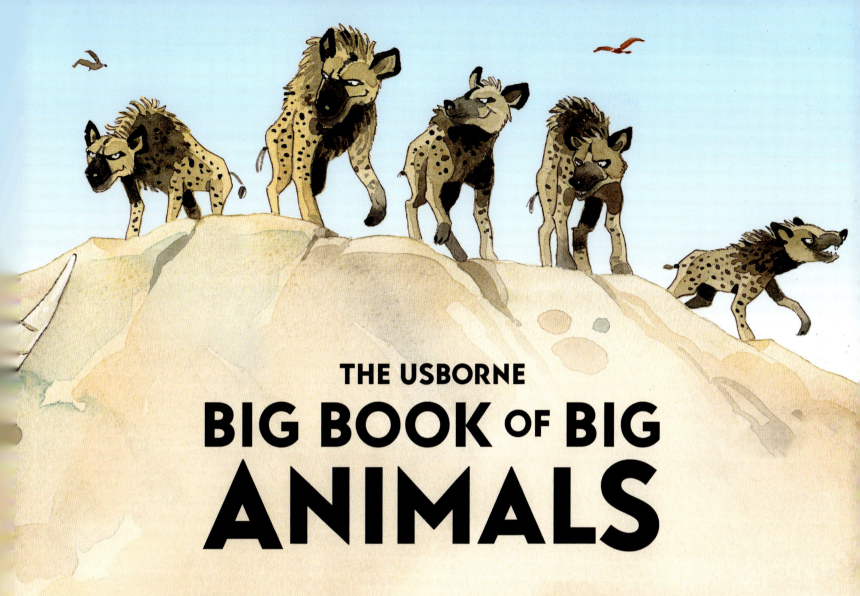

THE USBORNE
BIG BOOK OF BIG
ANIMALS

Written by Hazel Maskell

Illustrated by Fabiano Fiorin

Designed by Stephen Wright
Edited by Alex Frith
Animal experts: Dr. John Rostron and Dr. Margaret Rostron

Series designer: Mary Cartwright Series editor: Jane Chisholm
Additional design by Lisa Verrall
Image manipulation by John Russell

How big is BIG?

Some animals are very TALL. Some are very LONG. Others are very HEAVY.

Elephants are the heaviest land animals. Some weigh more than 70 people put together.

Elephant tusks are very long teeth.

The biggest animal of all

The blue whale is the biggest animal that has ever lived – even bigger than the biggest dinosaur.

Whales come up to the surface to breathe air through these breathing holes.

The largest blue whales weigh more than a medium-sized plane, and are close to 30m (100 feet) long – longer than a tennis court.

The biggest whales eat tiny living things that float in the water. Sometimes, the amount they eat in a day adds up to the weight of a hippopotamus.

A blue whale's tongue alone is as heavy as an elephant.

Its mouth can hold enough water to fill 400 bathtubs.

Andean condors' wings can stretch over 3m (10 feet) from tip to tip.

An ostrich's neck is around 1m (3 feet) long.

Ostriches are the biggest of all birds. The largest grow taller and heavier than an average person.

Ostrich chick

An ostrich can't fly, but it can cover up to 5m (16 feet) with each step it takes.

Dangerous animals

Most of these animals are fierce hunters, but three of the biggest — hippos, buffalo and rhinos — only eat plants. But they're so big they can easily trample on other animals.

Hippopotamus
Length: some are over 5m (16 feet) long
Weight: some are over 3,600kg (8,000lbs)
Hippos spend up to 16 hours a day wallowing in water.

Spotted hyena
Shoulder height: up to 90cm (3 feet)
Weight: up to 85kg (190lbs)
Hyenas aren't cats or dogs. Their closest relatives are small animals called civets.

Jaguar
Length: up to 2m (6 feet)
Weight: up to 160kg (350lbs)
Jaguars have the strongest bite of any cat.

Lion
Length: some are over 3m (10 feet) long
Weight: up to 250kg (550lbs)
Lions are the only cats that live and hunt in groups.

- Black bear
- Grizzly (brown) bear

Bear
Shoulder height: often over 1m (3 feet)
Weight: up to 1,000kg (2,200lbs)
Grizzly bears and polar bears are the largest animals that hunt on land.

Komodo dragon
Length: some are over 3m (10 feet) long
Weight: up to 160kg (350lbs)
Komodo dragons are the biggest lizards.

African buffalo
Length: some are over 3m (10 feet) long
Widest horn span: over 1m (3 feet)
African buffalo live in herds of up to 2,000.

Rhinoceros
Length: up to 4m (13 feet)
Rhinos are the second biggest land animals, after elephants.

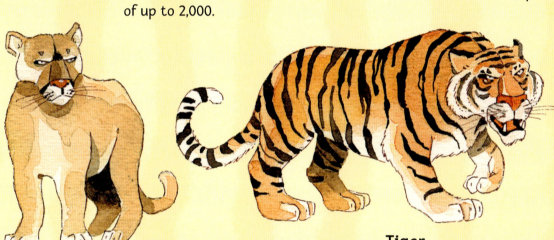

Puma
Length: up to 2m (6 feet)
Weight: up to 100kg (230lbs)
Pumas can leap over five times their height up off the ground.

Tiger
Length: up to 3m (10 feet)
Weight: up to 300kg (660lbs)
Tigers are the longest, heaviest cats of all.

Leopard
Length: up to 2m (6 feet)
Weight: up to 90kg (200lbs)
Most leopards are yellow with black spots, but some are black all over.

Crocodile
Length: up to 7m (23 feet)
Weight: up to 1,500kg (3,300lbs)
Some crocodiles have as many as 70 teeth.

King cobra
Length: up to 5m (16 feet)
Height: they can rear up over 1m (3 feet)
King cobras are the biggest poisonous snakes.

Anaconda
Length: up to 8m (26 feet)
Weight: up to 200kg (440lbs)
Anacondas are the heaviest snakes.

The tallest **grizzly bears** are over 3m (10 feet) tall when they're standing – that's way too tall to fit through an average doorway.

Polar animals

Big animals live all around the world – even in the freezing lands and oceans around the North and South Poles.*

Lynx
Length: over 1m (3 feet)
Weight: can get close to 40kg (90lbs)
Lynxes can hunt animals more than three times heavier than they are.

Moose
Length: some are over 3m (10 feet) long
Shoulder height: up to 2m (6 feet)
Moose are the biggest deer of all.

Polar bear
Length: up to nearly 3m (10 feet)
Weight: can be over 680kg (1,500lbs)
A polar bear's top swimming speed is 10km/h (6mph).

Antarctic fur seal
Length: up to 2m (6 feet)
Weight: up to 210kg (460lbs)
Males have a long mane, with thick fat and muscles underneath.

Leopard seal
Length: some are over 3m (10 feet) long
Weight: up to 540kg (1,200lbs)
Of all seals, leopard seals are the fiercest hunters. Some even hunt other seals.

Walrus
Length: some are over 3m (10 feet) long
Weight: up to 2,000kg (4,400lbs)
Walruses are much bigger than all seals, except elephant seals.

*The symbol by each animal shows whether it lives in the North or the South.

The heaviest **moose** weigh more than three reindeer put together.

The biggest moose's antlers can get close to 2m (6 feet) across.

Emperor penguins raise their chicks in colder conditions than any other birds – as cold as -60°C (-76°F).

These wings are called flippers. They are used for swimming, not flying.

Biggest, fastest, heaviest...

Ostriches lay the biggest eggs. The largest weigh more than 20 hens eggs.

Hen's egg

The biggest butterfly is the **Queen Alexandra's birdwing**. It's wider than a dinner plate.

Cheetahs are the fastest land animals. They can run at over 100km/h (60mph).

Australian pelicans have the biggest beaks of any bird – they hold more water than a large watering can.

...it's a **colossal squid**.

Colossal squid have the biggest eyes of any animal – they are bigger than bowling balls.

Experts think the biggest **colossal squid** may grow to over 13m (43 feet) long – though no one has ever seen one that big.

This bird weighs about as much as a 4-year-old child.

The heaviest flying bird is the **great bustard**.

The tallest dog is the **Great Dane**.

The biggest Great Danes are as tall as a Shetland pony.

A chihuahua is about as tall as a can of beans.

The biggest hunter is the **sperm whale**. It grows much longer than a bus, and hunts huge animals including colossal squid.

Usborne Quicklinks

For links to exciting websites about animals with videos and activities, scan the QR code or go to usborne.com/Quicklinks and type in the keywords "big animals".

Usborne Publishing is not responsible for the content of external websites. Children should be supervised online. Please follow the online safety guidelines at usborne.com/Quicklinks

This edition first published in 2025 by Usborne Publishing Limited, 83-85 Saffron Hill, London EC1N 8RT, United Kingdom. usborne.com Copyright © 2025, 2017, 2010 Usborne Publishing Limited. The name Usborne and the Balloon logo are registered trade marks of Usborne Publishing Limited. All rights reserved. No part of this publication may be reproduced, stored in a retrieval system or transmitted in any form or by any means without prior permission of the publisher. First published in America 2010. This edition first published 2025. UE.